AF226133

To The youth of the world; Imagine,
inspire, invest and enjoy.

Once upon a time in a typical town, located somewhere in some typical state, there once lived a young girl named Aaliyah with innate traits. Aaliyah was roughly five years old and was very passionate about learning.

So one day while it was still very early in the morning and Aaliyah's parents were still asleep, she awoke in her bed in her room that she shared with her older sister, Rihanna, with a desire to feed her passion and find something to do.

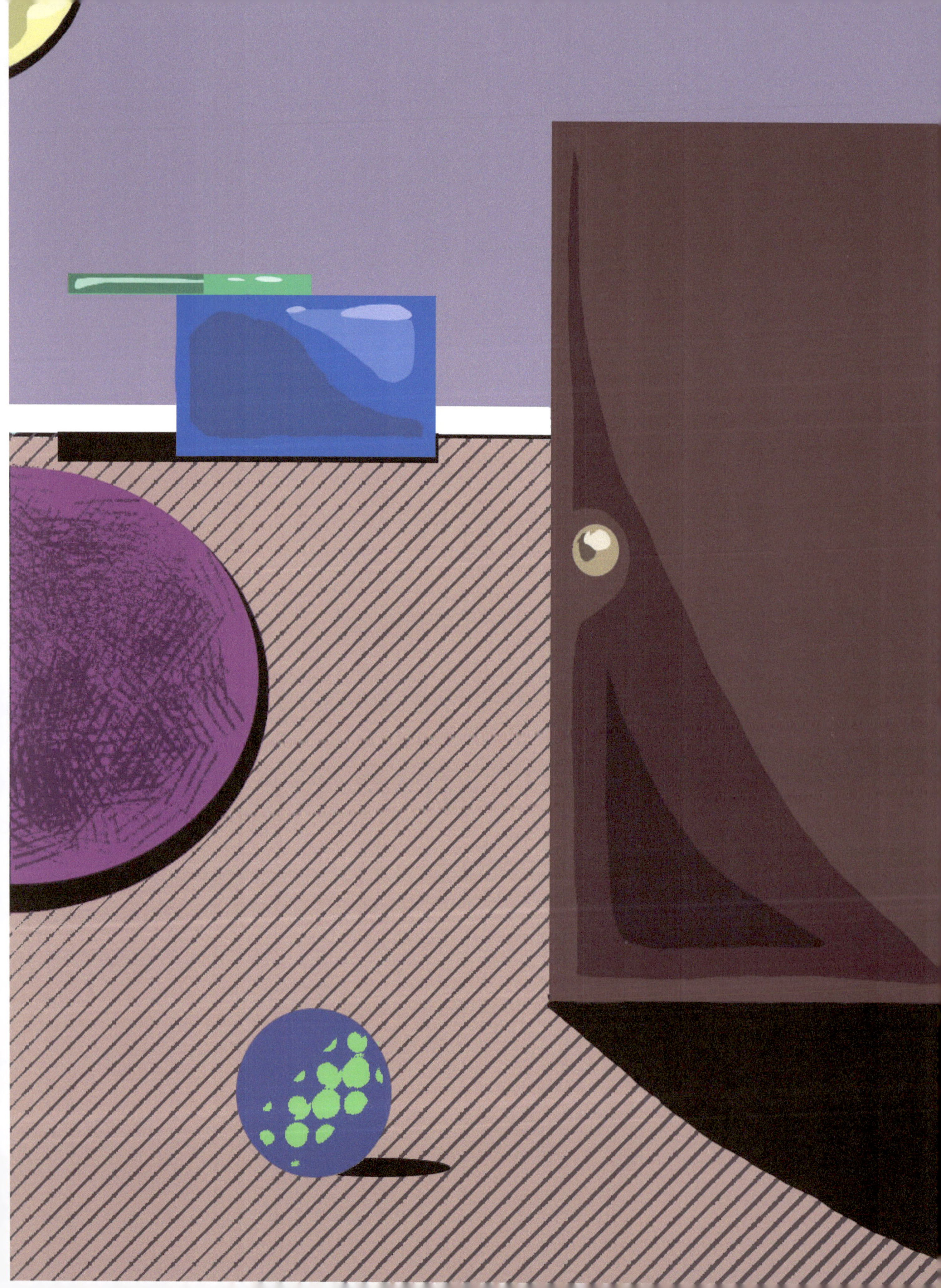

Open minded and motivated, Aaliyah thought on what to do with her day. What could she learn? Go outside? Maybe. What could she do? Run! Possibly. So many questions came into her mind.

She then thought of a wonderful idea. She wanted to learn more about hygiene. She could do this through the practicing and application of important steps that teach, promote and create the conditions for good personal hygiene. Then, conclude the lessons with reading more about hygiene from a book on her family's bookshelf.

Aaliyah then began to think about what she already knew about good daily personal hygiene from her parents. Those memories included taking baths, washing her hands after bathroom use, brushing her teeth, combing her hair, and putting on fresh, clean clothes.

Aaliyah was by far smart enough to start and finish her own bath however, she preferred the help of her older sibling, Rihanna, so she yelled out her name loudly until she replied, "Sure, I'm coming!".

For Aaliyah's family the various things to help with personal hygiene and maintain cleanliness were stored away neatly in a shelved closet. Items such as shampoo, conditioner, body lotion, hand sanitizer, toothpaste, towels, rags, and combs or brushes.

Bath time was always a favorite moment of Aaliyah's.
She enjoyed playing in the water with the bubbles
that were floating in her bath. To complete her
full bath routine, Aaliyah followed a few simple steps.

First, she soaked in the bath water and located the soap.
Next, she lathered her rag that she intended to wash up with in
lots of soap and then scrubbed her entire body with the soapy
rag. After that, she rinsed off all the soap from her wet body.
Finally, she got out of the bath water and dried off her
body with a clean, soft towel. Aaliyah would often repeat
the steps to washing up before drying off, but not on
this occasion.

Now she was clean and able to put on her orange slippers while wrapped in her favorite green towel; Aaliyah was ready to go on to the next activity in her hygiene routine. Brushing her teeth for fresh breathe and healthy gums. With a pea sized amount of children's toothpaste on her toothbrush, Aaliyah began with several small, controlled, repetitive brushing motions. She was sure to get every tooth, top to bottom, side to side, as well as front to back.

Aaliyah's journey then led her back to her room to get dressed into some fresh, clean clothes. She puts on underwear, since she is potty trained and finds her second favorite ballerina outfit to wear.

Finalliy dressed, Aaliyah moved on to the
final step of her hygiene adventure. Combing and arranging
her hair is fun to her and makes her feel better about herself.
Aaliyah used a mirror to make sure her hair was clean
and neat; She loves her hair texture. Coconut oil or shea butter
are things that are often added by her mother or sister to help
keep her hair soft and smelling good.

Completing her hygiene adventure at home that day, Aaliyah had a refreshed mindset and the chance to demonstrate what she had already known about hygiene. Still thirsty for knowledge, Aaliyah took things further by selecting a book from the bookshelf to read.

Capitivated and excited she quickly sat in the huge chair.
She looked at each page, sounded out all the letters, and read
all the words. Now it is so, that this story comes to a close;
As Aaliyah read more about hygiene, washing, getting in
between and showed you how to always stay clean.

The End.